THE
MOSES WITHIN

(The Urban Challenge)
For Youth

by

TRACY J. BROWN

www.urbanamericausa.org

authorHOUSE™

1663 LIBERTY DRIVE, SUITE 200
BLOOMINGTON, INDIANA 47403
(800) 839-8640
WWW.AUTHORHOUSE.COM

First published by AuthorHouse 11/18/05

ISBN: 1-4208-6673-7 (sc)

Library of Congress Control Number: 2005905517

Printed in the United States of America
Bloomington, Indiana

This book is printed on acid-free paper.

Contents

FOREWORD

It has been 139 years since the Emancipation Proclamation freed the slaves, and 39 years since Martin Luther King's contribution to America. Still, today, statistics show that as a group, Blacks continue to lead more difficult lives than any other group of people in America. That is why I say, Pharaoh, let my people go!

It is now time to stop blaming Pharaoh, and take responsibility for your own opportunities for advancement. The key is to extend yourself. Never let yourself stay in the comfort zone. Break out, set high goals and never settle for less. I speak from personal experience. I overcame unreasonable odds against me. Once I was able to see the success in my own life, I immediately wanted to share my blessings and help other people become successful.

Through the writing of this book my desire is to share with the world how FAITH, FAMILY, FELLOWSHIP AND FUNDAMENTAL FINANCE

KNOWLEDGE can transform the Urban Community. It is a joy, a natural high to see other people accomplish their goals. There is no time to loose, and no better place to start than with our youth.

INTRODUCTION
TRACY'S JOURNEY

Abandoned

As far as introductions go, this will be a long one, but it is an introduction to the soul of the person who wrote this book, and it will help you understand how, if I can do it, you can do it to.

I was conceived as a one-night stand. When I look back on how my life began, it reminds me of some aspects of Moses' life. (Exodus 2). The modern-day Pharaohs of America had exerted so much pressure, social and financial, on my mother, that this honest woman came to the very point of giving me away. Luckily, she considered adoption and not abortion, or I would not be writing this message to you today. I have never met my father. I was told he belonged to the 82nd Airborne in 1965, stationed at Pope Air force Base. I was told his name was David Simmons from Washington, D.C.

(If you ever happen to read this book, Dad, never worry about me, I'm doing great).

Rescued

As I said, approximately two months after my birth, my mother was ready to give me away. She wanted a better life for me, and she did not see any hope for me in what she considered her miserable existence. But God had a bigger plan. Just as my new parents were coming to pick me up, my grandmother walked in the door early, returning from a hard day of house-cleaning work. She asked my mother who the people outside were, and what they were waiting for. My mother broke the news that she was giving me away to a more stable family. Thank God for Grandma Ella Malloy being five minutes early or I would have been gone. My grandmother stated clearly to everyone involved that no grandchild of hers would ever be given away like a stray kitten. She refused to allow the exchange to take place. I believe that my mother resented the interference. Although she never admitted it, I am pretty convinced that I was being sold. From that day forward my main caretaker was my grandmother. She was a strong-willed lady who had lost her husband to illness when my mother was merely five years old. She was no stranger to hardship; she raised ten children with a third grade education. In my eyes, however, she had a Ph.D. in Wisdom.

My grandma, Ella Jane Malloy, was born in 1908. She would repeatedly tell me that I could work miracles. It was her absolute confidence in my ability that ultimately inspired me to pursue my dreams. Regardless of what my dreams and goals would be, all I knew was that my grandmother said I would be the "miracle in our family". I do not attempt to understand why my childhood was so complex, or why I have always been passionate about helping those who are emotionally, financially and spiritually bankrupt. My interpretation is that God was preparing me to be a leader for the urban community. In my hours of doubt I would ask questions. Lord, could I be the one you are calling? This kid, raised in poverty by a single parent who did not want her own child? A kid that was placed in special education classes, labeled as the least likely to succeed? A young man who made a 600 on the SAT and does not have a college degree? Lord are you sure I can lead the people? What will I say to the people? Whom will I say sent me?

Every time I asked these questions, I was filled with the belief that, Yes! My life can be utilized to help uplift the heart, mind and soul of many people who are hurting in our communities. Now, I respectfully clarify that I am not trying to emulate Moses. I just believe God has called me just as he called Moses to lead the Israelites. There are many unspoken Moses quietly doing their good work among us. My call is to reach each and every one of you, to let you know that it is time for the Church, community leaders, the Government and all others to be like Moses and help free the Urban Community. That is why I refer to Moses appeal, he said, "Pharaoh, let my people go!"

I would also like to share with you the birth of my passion in the urban communities. To tell you the story I must take you back to Fayetteville North Carolina. About two weeks before my high-school graduation, the pillar of strength in my life, my grandmother, passed away. The day after graduation I was forced to move out from the 2-bedroom, 700 square feet cinderblock home that held so many memories for me. My grandmother had provided for us. She left my mom and me an insurance policy to help us get a head start in our lives in case anything happened to her. Since my mom was on welfare, my grandmother would always do what she could do to make sure her grandson would be taken care of. My mom wanted to take my little brother Robert and move south to Atlanta, Georgia. I did not follow them. I decided it was time for me to try and make something of myself. I was eighteen years old, and I made a commitment that I would never have to fall back on the welfare system again. I can still see in my mind's eye the last welfare check I received at the age of eighteen for $220. I couldn't wait to make it on my own. My mom, however, was not able to break away from the welfare mentality. We therefore made a difficult decision. We split the insurance money and went our separate ways. She took $250.00 and I took $250.00. My mother moved south to Atlanta Georgia, and went back to the welfare system. I stayed in Fayetteville, and went to work. Here I have to tell you a little about my neighborhood. I could have easily settled for the drug life; it was all around me. I went to school with the drug boys and played on the same teams. I had family members that where involved with drugs. However, I knew that was not the life. I knew I had to keep a clean heart, mind and soul. My grandmother had instilled so much confidence in me, and I could not let her down. Even after her death she continues to be my biggest earthly inspiration. Thank God for my grandmother.

Betrayed

What follows is a succession of steps that led me to the place I enjoy today, although at the time, these stages were neither easy nor fair. After working for a local drugstore and meeting all the requirements for a promotion promised once I graduated from high school, I was denied the position of merchandise manager that I had worked so hard for. Even though I had a sterling record, I was told that the problem was my age. At eighteen years old, the drugstore management feared that the older employees would not follow my leadership. I was flabbergasted. I was well respected and often called on for help from the other local stores. A long-time black employee stated to me that it was not in the district manager's best interest to hire me, because I was young, black and from the 'hood. This same district manager had told me that I would make a great manager; everyone new I was his rising star. However, I believe employee pressure persuaded him to betray his integrity and deny the well-deserved management position. I am telling you these details so that you can get an idea of my emotional state. At this point I was at the lowest I had ever been. I was away from my family. I had just lost my guardian angel, my grandmother. I had worked myself to the bone to get a promotion that was not only falsely promised but unjustly denied. I had no funds for college. I had no place to live. I barely made enough to rent a room. It was at this juncture that I took my first knowing step to pull myself away from the destiny that seemed unavoidable carved out for me. I had a taste of the life that my mother was living, moving from place to place, and I realized that before long I would get caught in the same vicious circle, or worse perhaps. I decided to make a drastic change. Although it had never been in my future plans, I joined the U.S.Navy.

Determined

I entered into the Navy on a freezing January day, 1985, in Great Lakes. I woke up the very next morning with the absolute certainty that the military life was not for me. Since I had a three-year term ahead of me, I made the best of it. I began to learn about different cultures and people from all walks of life. I realized the military could not offer me the dreams I desired for my grandmother and me, but that I would use the opportunity to design a better life once I had completed my service. I juggled several different alternatives. I remember that my first possible choice was to stay in the military and become an officer. Towards that goal I began to take college preparatory courses at a local community college. The next logical step was to apply for the Naval Academy. With a prior SAT score of 600 from high school, I did not meet the entry requirements. So I began to work hard by taking remedial college preparatory courses. I became obsessed with developing my basic reading and grammar skills to the point that I would spend all my spare time reading and studying basic grammar books. I would go to the library daily during my lunch break, and would study one new word in the dictionary daily. I even went as far as studying how my grandma taught me. I would sleep with the book under my pillow. I think the only reason this system worked was because I believed it did.

I share these details with you because I suspect that some of you are going through the same trials that I encountered in my youth. One of the biggest obstacles I had to surmount was my inability to communicate properly. I was self-conscious because I knew that my English level was probably equivalent to the tenth grade. I was afraid that people would think less of me for that reason. I was by no means an isolated occurrence. Fifty percent of all African-American inmates in prison do not have a high-school education. This heart-breaking statistic is a convincing indication that one of the main origins of their perpetual turmoil is that they lack of communications skills that are indispensable to get ahead. They do not know how to relate to society. They don't know the code. So they are shut out and consequently they react with violence. They hold all this anger in and later they explode into the wrong lifestyle. I managed to survive, it's only by the grace of God. Looking back at my early schooling, I have to say that the bussing system in my case worked, because it gave me the opportunity to attend school in a higher income neighborhood and make friends with children from a more privileged background. The self-confidence that my Grandmother's wisdom had instilled in me made me recognize that these children where no smarter than me. They were just lucky to have had more exposure to education and a stronger family support structure. Most of them had two-parent families. I was morbidly embarrassed about poverty. I would not let them know how poor I really was. Whenever my friend's parents offered to give me a ride home, I would ask them to drop me off at my aunt's house, because her house looked slightly better than ours. I got away with it; I don't know that they ever realized the severity of my reality. I was poor, but I had enough pride to do my best with what I had at my disposal. I had pride but I still was too shameful of my living conditions.

My memories of the house we lived in are usually connected to the hardships we endured. It was a very small two-bedroom cinderblock house. and it got so cold in the wintertime that we could not take baths (we had to wash with a wash pail in the living room with a kerosene heater). The summer was not any easier. It would get so awfully hot there that the only relief would be to put my head in the freezer from time to time, to get a breath of cool air. Once I became a teenager, I would spend my summer days and weekends at the mall. Ironically, people thought that the attraction for me to go to the mall was a young girl. I let them think that, because I didn't want to admit the real reason. The mall was a great way to keep cool. But my memories of that house are also firmly connected to my memories of my grandmother. She was a strong lady, and proud enough to never complain. We couldn't afford to put in an air conditioning unit, and we certainly couldn't afford any increase in the electricity bill. So my grandmother would just say that air-conditioning was not required, there was nothing wrong with the Lord's air; as simple as that. On countless occasions Grandma would run short on money for food. I remember coming down to the last single can of noodle soup. I remember very well what that can look like. There was a kind black lady name Ms. Georgia who had a store. She would let us buy groceries on credit because she knew that my grandmother always paid her back. Now that I am an adult, I am amazed and wonder how my grandma managed to stretch the money (and the food) so well. My grandmother's income consisted of the social security payment from her husband

and whatever she got paid for cleaning houses. After a whole week of housekeeping work, she would come back with twenty-five dollars. I am unable, still today, to figure out how someone could pay my grandmother so little, but this is the way we lived and this was the reality that my grandmother dealt with to raise me.

After all this talk about my grandmother, you are probably wondering what happened to my mother. I like to think that she was trying to find happiness. This was in the late 70's. She would go out and not come home for weeks. Lacking a father figure, I was desperately in need of her presence. But she would subject me to long periods of separation, probably unaware of the pain that it caused me. If you have children, please stay involved with their lives. There is no possible replacement for the security that the love of a parent gives a child. Even if you do not have custody, make it a priority to keep in touch with your children. I spent my entire childhood trying to figure out, "Why is my life so harsh?" Now I believe God was preparing me for this journey.

I am aware that each of us has to travel their own road, and will encounter their own stumbling blocks along the way. My childhood was harsh, but so are the childhoods of other millions of people. I will just mention a brief summary of my own trials, in the hope that you may identify with some of them and realize that there is always a way to lift yourself up and away from your circumstances. In my case, the lessons at different stages of my life that prepared me for my current journey were:

- Being born out of wedlock and almost being given away by my mother
- Moving constantly from one place to another
- The knowledge of the significance of that last can of soup in the house
- Surviving in a dangerous, drug infested neighborhood
- My mother being kidnapped
- Witnessed my mother's alcoholism almost every day
- Being whipped for asking for a meal
- Being beaten as a child when trying to help my mother fight off abusive men
- Worrying every time my mother walked out the door, that she would not come back

There it is. Just a short list sums up years of struggle and heartache. I'm in tears just writing this information. I have learnt, however, that in order to move pass my hurt and help others grow from their pain I must "Keep It Real." I often tell people how I received a B.A. from the School of Survival and a Ph.D. from Praising Him Daily. Throughout this book I will share with you how the entire childhood crisis equipped me to help make a difference.

Notes

PART ONE
UNLEASH THE MOSES WITHIN

I don't think I am anything special. I believe we all have a Moses-like character hidden within. It takes commitment to cultivate the desire to make a positive difference in our world, and I made that commitment. The fact that you are reading this book indicates to me that you are a person looking to make a positive difference. You have it in you to make the commitment. If you have not decided in which area you would prefer to make a difference, or where to employ your desire to help other people improve, I would urge you to consider working with our youth. I pray that one of the areas you commit time to making a positive impact is with our young people. If we do not invest the time today, then I am hesitant to predict what the future outcome will show.

We need *each one to reach one*. It is as simple as that. Our children's heritage will be the fruits of our labor today. And the same goes for our children's children, as the bible teaches. The best investment of our time is in any time invested in working with children all over the world. You cannot imagine what a little time invested could do for millions of troubled youth all over the world. For the last ten years of my life I have volunteered to speak at a local youth detention home. Basically, it is a youth jail that holds the kids there until their trial. I have spoken with hundreds of young men and women who have committed severe crimes such as car jacking, armed robbery, assault, drug trafficking and even murder. One of the first things that amazed me when I started working at the center, is how you cannot tell the difference in a child who has skipped school versus the child who has committed a serious crime. I believe that children do not commit these cruel crimes out of evil. Kids who commit these crimes are not born bad. Most of them have lacked proper guidance in their early years. They are crying out for help, leadership and love. Without a strong positive role model a child will gravitate to any influence that is in their surroundings. Unfortunately the world has plenty of violence on television, in music, in entertainment and, of course, in the streets. It is extremely easy for a child to get caught up in what I call the "mix". The mix becomes the lifestyle. It can start at a very young age and it will quickly shape the child's life to its environment.

The Mix

What is this "mix" like? What does it do? Imagine you are standing at the edge of a pool. The pool is filled with what looks like water. The liquid is clear enough that it allows you to see the bottom. This pool represents the world we live in. When you stand beside the pool, looking in, you can see clearly. But once you jump into the pool, and start wading, you can't see the bottom any longer. Things become blurred. Imagine if the liquid that you jumped in is not water, but very heavy oil, that makes it hard to move and breathe. Life in the mix is the same way. While you are standing on the side, it looks like everything will be easy, and you will be able to keep it under control. You think you can see what is going on in the world until you jump in. It becomes increasingly difficult to move, as the density of the world starts to encircle you and confine you. If you are a young person or an adult reading this book, you may have a good idea of what I am talking about. It may have seemed easy and then it got really complicated. I'm here to show you a way out of the pool, back to safer ground.

But how do we fall into the mix? Let us start from early childhood. As soon as you are born into this world, you start looking for reference points to find out how to behave in it. You look to your parents, or the adults that are taking care of you. You imitate their actions, and their every gesture. This is how you learn to walk, talk and even to smile. Some of us are forced to grow up without our parent's guidance. Unfortunately, this leaves a gap open, it makes us vulnerable. We attempt to follow whomever shows up to fill in the void that our parents have left. In my case, I was fortunate to have my Grandmother step into that role. But for many other people, who are not so fortunate, the reality can be quite different. One of the trickiest aspects of the mix, is that people that get lost in it look for relief by bringing other people down with them. So if you are a child that lacks the guidance of a parent, you may be unfortunate enough to fall under the sphere of influence of the mix.

Let's say this has happened to you. You have been brought down into the mix by someone who was supposed to be your role model. You are in elementary school in the mix and you hit your first brick wall. You get in trouble for fighting. You naturally do not understand why you where punished. Why? Fighting seems natural to you because it is the behavior you have been taught. Because you are now caught up in the mix you cannot see no farther than your nose. Remember the pool? You have tried to open your eyes under the water, but you can no longer see clearly. It is the same in the life process of the mix. If you are lucky to be able to go back to your parents for guidance, or, my case, to my grandmother, you will have a way to tell the difference between what you are doing and the right thing. But this can only happen if you have a positive role model to compare your behavior to. You need guidance to see where you are going. You need someone to tell you how to go back up for air in the pool. Unfortunately, with the lack of role models, our black youth today are often guided by the life of the streets. Let us go to the next level.

You are now in high school and you hit another brick wall in the mix. It could be that you are pregnant or have made someone pregnant, or that you are involved with drugs, failing school, in jail or have actually taken a life. The sad point now is that you do not understand why everyone is so furious. Because you are scared and confused, you turn against everyone who is trying to help you. If your parents are around, you may have developed a dislike for them. You cannot understand why everyone is so hard on you. You do not understand because you are caught up in the mix. So what do you do for comfort? You seek friends who can relate to you. You can relate to them because they are also caught up in the mix. This perpetuates the cycle. These are the same people you call your "peeps" and you are willing to die for. You sometimes have your gang banging friends or relatives who you love more than yourself and your family.

Why do you have such allegiance to them? It is because you both share the same challenge. Both are caught up in the mix. They cannot help you get out of the mix because they don't know the way out, or else they would be the first to get out. It is not good policy to ask a person for help who is worse off than yourself. With that in mind let us get back to your mix life during your teenage years.

As we said before, you are in high school caught up in the mix, but you have escaped so many traumatic situations and you have lived in the mix so long, that you have began to take pride in the lifestyle. Because it is so hard to get out, you begin to program yourself to believe that "only the strong can survive." You are to blind to the next brick wall that you inevitably come to when you live in the mix. This brick wall can take different shapes, but it is unavoidable. It could be death, prison for life, death row or brain death from drugs. If you know of someone that has hit the final brick wall, please find charity in your heart. If you know of someone who needs to get out of the mix, then there is still time. I plead to you to share the life changing process that I will share with you in this book, and that I have shared with thousands of young people each year.

The solutions that I will share with you will consist of some daily applications that I believe can make a major impact in your desire to change. Keep in mind that this practical information is not something I just heard. I have lived through them. I am probably alive because of them. These are successful principles that have transformed my life. It taught me a new thought process. I personally say to you, 'If I can do it, you can too." My prior life of feeling hopeless, homeless, poor, abandoned, lost was replaced by success, joy and hope. Need I say more? You cannot keep making excuses for not trying to improve your life. Your childhood could not have been much worse than mine. Like the old saying goes," I've been there and done that."

Notes

PART TWO
A PRACTICAL PLAN FOR
YOUR LIFE: "TRACY'S KIDS"

Let me tell you a little anecdote. In 1992 I was reading an article by the Drug Enforcement Agency in Washington, D.C. The article stated how bad the drug problem was among young poor urban youth. They did not have a solution on how to deal with the problem. I was enraged at the careless way in which the article was written. It was unjustly labeling poor inner city kids. Being from the inner city myself, I did not agree with their philosophy. These people did not know, and they definitely needed to know. I decided to take action. I immediately wrote a letter to Washington to explain how I was raised in the environment that was misrepresented in the article. I explained how I lived around crime, drugs and violence, and how that life style did not shape my life pattern. I told them I had a solution for the problem described in the DEA article.

The White House gave me an appointment to share with them my national plan. I then presented my plan to the White house about how to develop a role model for inner city children. This role model must be a person that our youth can look up to as a leader. We have role models in different fields, in music, in athletics, in sports, in science. But who is the positive Black Role model for our communities? When I asked this question, the room became silent. The Federal Government began to share with me the national budget and what the cost would be to promote a real person role model in the inner city community. I was frustrated after I saw that there was not enough money allocated to help one city, let alone helping every inner city in the United States.

Since by now you know me a little better, you will not be surprised if I tell you that this obstacle actually made me go back home motivated to develop my own plan. I had to come up with a strategy that would be accepted by inner city children, and a plan that would allow youth to be role models for each other. Additionally, this program had to be a hip and trendy program that the kids liked. At the time there was some famous black kids on television who where not positive. Their motto was, "we don't die, we multiply." I said if we can have a program for bad kids we could have one for Positive Kids. And this is how "**Tracy's Kids**" was created.

When I designed the program I set up a strategy to allow each child to teach a child. Tracy's Kids' oath is a memorization message that can be taught from youth to youth. Once a child learns this tongue twister, he or she then becomes a "Certified Tracy's Kid". The next child must now recite it to be a certified Tracy's kid, and so it continues. The idea is that once the program gets rolling, each youth become role models for each other. Just bear with me for a moment and it will all start to make sense. The oath goes like this...

"TRACY'S KIDS OATH OF COMMITMENT TO EXCELLENCE"

- ONE LIFE
- TWO BASIC BELIEFS (Believe in self and tomorrow is a better day)
- THREE LIFE LONG LOVES (Love all mankind, family and self)
- FOUR CHAIR LEGS OF SUCCESSFUL LIVING (physical, emotional, spiritual and financial)
- FIVE PROMISING PRINCIPLES TO PRODUCE WEALTH AND HAPPINESS (Specifically define what you want, Dreams, Beliefs, Action, and Persistence)
- SIX SINCERE TRACY'S KIDS WHO SHARE

SUCCESS WITH SEVERAL SUCCESS
SEEKERS
- · SEVEN SENSATIONAL SYSTEMATIC
  DAYS OF PERSISTENCE WILL CREATE
  UNLIMITED SUCCESS
- EIGHT MILLION MOTIVATED TRACY'S
  KID'S WHO MIRACULOUSLY MOVE THE
  WORLD
- NINE TIMES A DAY TRACY'S KIDS WILL
  SAY, "I WILL WIN. WHY? I'LL TELL
  YOU WHY; BECAUSE I HAVE FAITH,
  COURAGE, AND ENTHUSIASM!"

Once children are certified, they receive
their "diploma":

The Success Code of Excellence

Hereby Recognizes:

(your name here)

For Having Successfully Learned Tracy's Kids Oath of Excellence

Date: _____

Notes

The following principles are the backbone of the program, and they are the philosophy behind each of the items in the oath.

TRACY'S KIDS PRINCIPLES

To help children understand some of the more complex principles I ask them to think of four chairs. I call them the Four Chairs of Life. I ask them to visualize four chairs in a single file placed next to each other, and I number them from left to right, one through four.

1. Then I tell them that the chair to the far left, Chair 1, is the chair of **assurance.** This chair represents a person who loves their self and, if they are Christian, they also show love for Christ. The person in this chair realizes that they are not perfect and they are always willing to try to improve until they succeed.
2. The next chair from left to right is Chair 2. This chair represents a person who is **insecure.** They are

like a chameleon, often telling lies
to disguise themselves in order to
get what they want. They may smile
one minute, and stab you in the back
the next. In the church this person is
called a hypocrite. They are a faithful
Christian on Sunday, and will curse you
on Monday. This person is always out
to step over you to get ahead.

3. The next chair is Chair 3, this person is
   a wannabe, and they are **not sure** who
   they are. They normally almost always
   fall to peer pressure, they lack the
   ability to think for self. This person in
   the church normally comes to church
   occasionally. They are searching for
   guidance. Chair 2 is a bad example for
   this person. This person will normally
   follow anything that feels right.

4. The last chair is number 4. This
   person does not care about anything
   or anyone. This person is mad about
   life and thinks everyone else is the
   problem. In the church this person
   normally is very negative and just
   comes to church to spew out their
   negative agenda.

Throughout my discussion of the Tracy's
Kid's Oath I often refer back to these four
chairs of life, to ask children who they are and

where they want to be. The choice is up to each one of them.

One Life

I tell the children that God only gave us one physical body and we must learn to respect how we use and abuse it. You are probably aware, as I am, of the large number of our youth that are having sex without protection and doing drugs at an alarming rate. These behavior patters expose them to diseases such as Hepatitis or Aids. A fast spreading disease like Aids can wipe out an entire generation of young people in ten years or less. Aids is becoming an epidemic among our youth, especially so for African-Americans. We have not even mentioned addictions such as alcohol, cigarettes and cocaine. These kids are destroying their health, but they don't know it. They have not been educated to understand that once you get AIDS there is no cure. They don't know that when you destroy your brain cells with the abuse of drugs your body eventually will slow up the process of regenerating cells. If they hear the message, they are not able to understand what it *means*. We must learn to respect and cherish this body that we have.

Going back to our chairs, Chair 1 will always love and respect self. They will not fall to the lies of lust and drugs. Chair 2 will normally be involved sexually and be a heavy user of drugs. They have to have something to balance their emotions with the lies they tell. Chair 3 is confused and will try anything that a person of negative or positive influence tells them to do. This person normally gets with the wrong crowd and settles for chair 2 or 4. Chair 4 is the person who is already addicted to drugs and sex. They don't care about their self; they are merely focused on the moment. If they do not change their life expectancy is likely to be very short.

Next, I will share how you begin to strive for Chair 1.

Two Basic Beliefs

You must have a commitment of belief in thyself and belief that tomorrow always offers you a better day. I once heard a speaker say, "Beliefs are the foundation or our character." Where do your beliefs come from? It is my conviction that your beliefs come from your constant exposure to any specific environment. For example, if you have been around bad blue people all your life, you will develop a belief that all blue people are bad. Is that a true statement? Absolutely not! Try this:

Complete the phrase: Money doesn't grow on...

I'm sure you were able to fill in the blank. Yet why is it that almost everyone can complete this phrase? It is because we have heard the phrase in family conversations for generations.

So, this brings me to the next question. Can your belief system be changed? Absolutely. You have the ability to change your own beliefs. Many of us have beliefs that are holding us back. What are some beliefs that are holding you back? Take a moment and make a list of the beliefs that are keeping you from achieving your potential. For example, do you believe going to school is boring? Now that you have identified those negative beliefs, continue to collapse the negative belief with a positive belief. Every time you think about going to school replace the negative image with the idea that going to school equates to a successful career. Remember constant exposure to the new pattern will eventually destroy the old belief pattern. "The essence of belief is the establishment of a habit," said Charles S. Pearce. I remember as a child how my mom often scolded me with negative words such as, "you are no good" or "you are weak" and other stronger and more hurtful words. After a while you inevitably begin to believe that negative junk. Have you ever heard parents shouting and screaming cruel words to their children when they are angry? Words like "you can't do that" or "you are going to be just like your father" (or whoever is the demonized person in proximity). Our parents do not realize the effect those words had on our life. "Man is what he believes," said Anton Chekhov.

Regardless of your past, do you believe that you can achieve more? Chair 1 always has a strong belief in self, Chair 2 believes more in their deceiving attitude than self. They will always hide behind the games they play. It's like the person who lies so much until they believe their own lie. Chair 3 believes in everyone but self, they are confused about who or what they believe. Chair 4 is that hard person who has no belief in self or tomorrow. They say, "I don't care". They have no positive outlook about tomorrow. They sometimes would prefer to check out of this life entirely. That is why they always appear to be so bitter with the world. Nelson Mandela, a man who had an excuse to be bitter, chose a different belief pattern that had a positive impact on the world. What chair do you imagine that chair Nelson Mandela would sit in? This is a man who stayed in prison for 27 years and later become President of South Africa. He did not focus on the past, and he kept a positive outlook about the future. Next time you are faced with a negative belief pattern be like Nelson Mandela, and focus on a positive future.

Three Life-Long Loves

Love all mankind, family and self. That word. Love. What is love? Love means many things to different people. What does love mean to you? "Love is to admire from the heart; to admire is to love with the mind," said Theophile Gautier (1811-1872). One of the most difficult things to do is to love someone who has mistreated you. However, that is one of the tests I believe God puts before us. He wants us to represent and uphold his wonderful name. Can you imagine the type of love that Dr. Martin Luther King had in his heart to be able to endure all the hurt and pain? There is a word for it. This love is called *agape* love. Agape love is unconditional love. To give you an example of this type of love, we must remember how Martin Luther King, Jr. loved his enemy throughout all the hate crimes and physical abuse to Blacks in the 60's. Martin Luther King said, 'Love is the only force capable of transforming an enemy into a friend."

Today I believe we must learn to love all mankind regardless of the differences we may have such as religion, race, beliefs or gender. Keep in mind that any hatred you feel towards another person Is only holding you back. Many young people today are bitter because of their unwillingness to let go of the past. I had to learn how to let go the negative past in my life or else I would never have the ability to see the future. We cannot look behind and look ahead at the same time. There was a story told about an African boy who was swimming in a lake and a snapping turtle grabbed his big toe and would not let go. After hours of pulling and stretching they where able to stretch the turtles neck enough to cut off the turtle's neck to free the boys toe. The turtle lost its life. The morale of the story is that the turtle lost its life because it was unwilling to let go. The lesson for you to remember is that you must let go of the past. If people could let go of their past I believe we would see less people on drugs, crime, and violence. The black population of our prison system would drastically drop.

Going back to our chairs once more, the person in Chair 1 has learned to love God, Self, Family and all mankind. Chair 2 loves only self and is not concerned with anyone else, they are self-serving. Chair 3 does not love self; they are searching for someone and something to love. This person is dangerous to self and society. Chair 4 has no clue about love, does not want to be loved, they are bitter about the past and they are afraid to move into the future.

Let go of the past and learn to love in the future. "Take away love and our earth is a tomb," said Robert Browning (1812-1889)

Four Chair-Legs of Successful Living

Since we were talking about chairs, let's imagine a chair with four legs. Each leg represents an aspect of successful living:

physical, emotional, spiritual and financial. First we must understand that for any chair to have a solid foundation it must have four good legs. We know if one of the legs on the chair is weak, or falls, the chair will be unstable and tilt over. Our lives work in the same way. I believe our life must be balanced like a chair with four legs that represent four essential areas of our life. Physical, Emotional, Spiritual and Financial. If one of those areas in your life is unstable your life chair will lean. For example, you can make all the money in the world. However, if you do not take care your physical body, and you become sick, the money will do you no good. We must strive to have all areas balanced to have a successful life. The tabloids are filled with story after story of famous people who have fallen because they could not find balance. What happened to those people who have achieved great fame or fortune? They seemed to have it all, but they all had a weak emotional leg. They resorted to drugs or other addictions, or had emotional challenges that did not allow them to form a stable family. My heart breaks when I hear about so many young black children who have lost their lives to selling drugs, all for that quick payday. They did not realize the money would not balance their life. It is too late for them but not for you. The key is to develop a plan that will provide you the desires of your heart within a balanced life.

"If you make money your god, it will plague you like the devil", said Henry Fielding (1707-1754).

Let's look at Chair1; they understand that life must be balanced. They understand that it takes more than finances to have a successful life. Chair 2 will normally be leaning on the emotional leg of life; with their inconsistent personality it will be only a matter of time before the chair falls. Chair 3 is most likely to be dependent on drugs; their life is an emotional roller coaster. Chair 4 is not spiritual; he hates living and does not trust anyone.

Five Promising Principles to Produce Wealth and Happiness

I shared with you some of my early experiences as an employee, a student and a navy recruit. Later on in my career, I had the good fortune of meeting a successful businessman who not only saw potential in me, but also shared the principles that had formed the basis of his success. He told me that if I followed these five principles, I would succeed in anything I set my heart and mind to. I am giving this wealth of information to you in the hope that you will be open to receiving these five principles that are essential to make any change in your life. They truly work.

STEP 1 -Specifically Define What You Want

Most people never get what they want out of life because they do not know what it is they really want. If you ask someone what they want, nine times out of ten you get the reply, "I want to be happy". But what does it mean? Being happy to me may mean having a loving family and being surrounded by friends, being happy to a scientist may mean devoting his work to something that will improve the lives of others, so you can see how the same word can mean very different things to different people.

In order for this principle to work, you have to define what you want in great detail. If you are in school, you should specifically determine the type grades you desire to have, how you plan to change to make the grades, when you plan to have the grades and then the biggest question to answer is why you desire those grades.

What *specific* plans could you start on today to improve some key areas in your life?

STEP 2 – Never Stop Dreaming

Michelangelo said, "The greater danger for most of us lies not in setting our aim too high and falling short; but in setting our aim too low, and achieving our mark." As children, it is very easy to dream. Think of Christmas. We dream about a bicycle, or having a swimming pool. As we grow we loose our ability to dream. We tend to be "realistic". Our daily occupations do not leave time for dreaming. It is a shame.

Your dreams will be the foundation of your goals. Now as you began to redirect your life we need to focus on the dreams you have for the future. It has been a life-long dream for me to write this and reach out and help others. I have seen my dream come true. Oh! What a feeling when you accomplish your dreams!

"I like the dreams of the future better than the history of the past." said Thomas Jefferson. This is a man who had a dream. Just like so many other illustrious people had a dream. They did not just wake up one morning and decided that they would be president, or write a book, or invent the telephone. They worked on their dream every day, defining it and molding it with their every thought. Write down your dreams and goals. Keep in mind these are dreams. Therefore, do not spare a thought, the sky is the limit. Please remember to be specific. Now, for the next 21 days focus on those dreams and goal. It takes a person approximately 21 days of consistency to develop any new habit. Develop the habit to dream.

STEP 3 – Believe

We have talked about beliefs before. We explained how beliefs are taught, and that by their very nature, they can be changed. Therefore, lets discuss some basic ideas on how to change your beliefs.

First of all, you have to change your environment. If your friends are going down the wrong path, you need to consider distancing yourself from them. At least for the time being. The time may come when you can come back and help them, but not until you have performed the change for yourself first. You must surround yourself with people who possess the traits that you are seeking to incorporate in your life. If you cannot find a person that you can follow and talk to in person, you can read about the lives and work of those type of individuals. Since I never knew my father, I grew up with no male figure in my home as a child. I had to seek male role models in books. My favorite was the late Martin Luther King, Jr. I'm became obsessed with reading and hearing more about his contributions. I began to pattern my life after him. As I got older I exposed myself to other great leaders whom I thought where examples of the life I desired.

STEP 4 – Take Action

What gets between us and our dreams is fear. How does one begin to transform their fears into action? I believe that when you do what you fear most, you conquer that fear. I have learned to ask myself two important questions when I am presented with a challenging situation. The first question is, "In this situation what is the worst that can happen to me?" The second question follows, "What is the best that can happen to me?"

In order to take action one must also believe or have faith that the action taken is *appropriate* for that situation.

STEP 5 – Persevere

Michelangelo said, "I saw the angel in the marble and carved until I set him free." Be persistent. We all have an angel inside. Your persistence will be driven by your desire to change.

Six Sincere Tracy's Kids Who Share Success With Several Success-Seekers

Over the last ten years of sharing Tracy's Kid's program, it is my experience that only approximately six young people out of one hundred fifty participants will sincerely get what I am saying. I will never forget a blonde thirteen-year-old boy at the detention home who walked up to me after my presentation and said, "I understand what you are saying, and I'm going to change from this moment forward". The following month I returned to the home, and the counselors informed me that this lovely boy had died in his cell. He had broken his neck. Although it was labeled an accident, I still wonder if he was tired of life and just killed himself. It may have been that he received the right message, at the wrong time. Maybe it was a day too late for him.

Consider making that change today because no one knows what tomorrow may bring. If you are reading this book it is likely that you will be one of the six who will commit to making a change.

"It is the most unhappy people who most fear change," said Mignon McLaughlin.

Seven Sensational Systematic Days of Persistence Will Create Unlimited Success

'It is not necessary to hope in order to undertake, nor to succeed in order to persevere," Charles the Bold (1433-1477)

My heart goes out to you. I know it will take an all-consuming commitment to make a positive impact in your life. I know it, because I have been through it. In my life I have learned that you must be ready to win. That's right. It may not be something you have thought about, because we tend to focus on our problems rather than our opportunities. But you actually have to make yourself ready for success, whenever it comes, seven days a week, 24 hours a day. You must be in it to win it. Get in the game now, and win it.

I look forward to hearing about your success in the near future.

Eight Million Motivated Tracy's Kids Who Miraculously Move the World

I have a dream that Tracy's Kid's will collectively reach over 8 million young people in ten years. I started this vision in 1992. Now, twelve years later I'm still on the battlefield. I probably have reached only one hundred thousand. But with this book and today's Internet capabilities I can see my goal of eight million coming true over the next five years. I maybe off track of my goal but it do not really matter because I am right on track for making a difference. You may not always achieve your goal on time but you can always keep your goal within reach.

Nine Times a Day Tracy's Kids Will Say: "I Will Win. Why? I'll Tell You Why. Because I Have Faith, Courage, and Enthusiasm!"

If you want to be a success in changing you present life I believe you have to set yourself up to win daily. And the best way to do that is program your self everyday for success. A great way to do this is every morning before you start your day to empower yourself with some daily affirmations. This is something I learn to do for myself and my children. I tell my 3-year-old son and my 6-year-old daughter, "You are beautiful black children, you are winners, you are achievers, you are God-fearing children, you are healthy, wealthy and brilliant. Daddy loves you and mommy loves you. You are loved." Just how I was programmed negatively as a child I can program myself and my children positively. I challenge you to remember to program yourself daily with the following affirmation;

I will win. Why? I'll tell you why. Because I have Faith, Courage and Enthusiasm.

Now that you have been introduced to how you can change your life the key will be for you to take action. Let's go back to the four chairs. Will you decide to stay in your chair or will you move to Chair 1. You see Chair 1 has made a commitment of change and is realizing true happiness. That is the first giant step. Are you ready? *Are you?*

If you like what you are reading but you are wondering where to start, let me help you. You start with first understanding that there will never be any true happiness in your life if you are lacking a relationship with Christ. Therefore, the first step will be accepting Christ as your savior. No, not just knowing that he exists. It is important that you first realize that you are a sinner. We all are. "For all have sinned and fall short of the glory of God." (Romans, 3:23) It is this sin that separates us from having a relationship with God. And God's only provision to bring us back to Him is through Jesus Christ. Jesus Christ died on the cross to pay the penalty for our sin and bridge the gap between God and us. "Jesus said...I am the way, and the truth, and the life; no one comes to the father, but through Me" (John14:6) Therefore, if you are ready to spend the remainder of your life in Chair 1, you can do it right now by realizing and *confessing* that you are a sinner. Ask God to *forgive* you and *save* you. Say those three things in a prayer, mean it from your heart and ask God to save you. You will be instantly advanced to Chair 1.

Once you are in Chair 1 you have a responsibility to study God's Word, to find a church home and remember this special moment when you accepted Christ as your savior. If you have accepted Christ on this day remember you sinful nature is still within you. However, you now will have knowledge that you are committing a sin. You now have a savior to pray for help, guidance, forgiveness and salvation.

Remember this day as your spiritual birthday!

On this _____ day of _____ in the year _____ ,I (your name here) accepted Christ as my savior.

Now, that your life has taken you on a new journey, what to do next?

As a new babe in Christ I often struggled. I wondered if I was staying on the right path. However, as I began to read the Bible, to pray and share in fellowship with other Christians, I was able to stay strong.

As my final gift to you in this book, I would like to leave you with the Three Basic Steps for a new Christian to grow in Christ. Follow them and enjoy your spiritual rebirth and share the good news with others.

1. **Pray**: your prayer life will be essential in your Christian walk.

2. **Read the Bible Daily**: as a new Christian it can be a challenge to interpret the Bible. Therefore, I will share with you some basic guidelines that helped me.

   • Read a chapter in Proverbs daily for the rest of your life. The book of Proverbs has 31 chapters and we have an average of 30 days in a month. For an example if today is the 5th of the month you will read the Fifth chapter of Proverbs. The Book of Proverbs Is all about wisdom. We all need wisdom.

   • Next, I challenge you to read the entire Bible in one year. If you start on January 1st and read an average of four chapters a night you can complete the Bible in one year. After several failed attempts, I finally accomplished the goal. If you fail, don't be discouraged. Just get right back to it. To get a good start read the New Testament first, you will find it easier to read.

3. **Find a good Bible-teaching church:** this means a church where the pastor actually preaches on what the scripture says. You should be able to follow along with the pastor's message from the Bible.

Did you find something in this book that inspired you? Please write me and share the good news at:

tracybrown@urbanamericausa.org

Your story can help many other people like you.

I look forward to hearing from you.

God Bless You!

Notes

ABOUT THE AUTHOR

Tracy J. Brown is President of First Providence Realty, Inc., located in Portsmouth, Virginia, a full service real estate company that specializes in Urban housing for low-to-moderate income families. Brown is the founder of the non-profit Urban America, USA, assisting housing authorities and faith-based organizations to develop community empowerment programs. He is the local president for National Association of Real Estate Brokers in Portsmouth, VA. Internationally, Brown has assisted with an urban community development project in Benin, West Africa, proposing construction of 1,100 new homes.

Brought up with scarce resources, Mr. Brown can share with authority the message of rising from adversity to prosperity with audiences of his radio show and motivational sessions. Mr. Brown speaks to Churches throughout the U.S on "Biblical Stewardship: Taking Back the Urban Community and

Community Empowerment." In Mr. Brown's upcoming book, " Tracy J. Brown The Moses Of Urban America," He will share a National Plan for the Black Church to take back The Urban Community. He is the Financial Comptroller of a 1,000-member church in Portsmouth, Virginia and a devoted father and husband.